The
PEARSON
Editing Exercises
Second Edition

Anna Ingalls
Southwestern College, Emeritus

Dan Moody
Southwestern College

Longman

New York Boston San Francisco
London Toronto Sydney Tokyo Singapore Madrid
Mexico City Munich Paris Cape Town Hong Kong Montreal

Ingalls/Moody, *Pearson Editing Exercises, Second Edition,*

Copyright ©2009 Pearson Education, Inc.

ISBN: 0-205-66618-3

1 2 3 4 5 6 7 8 9 10–BIR–11 10 09 08

CONTENTS

1A: Identifying Verbs

Directions: Underline the verbs in the following paragraph. In the space above each, label the verb *A* (action) or *L* (linking). Check to be sure that you have underlined the whole verb.

Example:

                                                     L

The Statue of Liberty in New York Harbor <u>is</u> the first thing that many

                     A

immigrants <u>see</u>.

Immigrants have made many important contributions to the United States of America. The Statue of Liberty honors them for their contributions. Even today, more than 35 percent of the eight million residents of New York City were born outside of the United States, and over 170 languages are spoken in the city. Over the years, New York has indeed been a city of opportunity and success for many immigrants. However, others live in poverty. New York City is the cultural capital of the United States. More book publishers and theater companies can be found in New York than in any other city in America. Several of the nation's most famous art museums are also located in New York. On the other hand, many thousands of New Yorkers live in substandard housing. In fact, almost one million New Yorkers receive income assistance from the government. Some of the richest and poorest people in our country are among the residents of the most famous part of the city, Manhattan.

1

1B: Distinguishing Between the Simple and the Complete Subject

Directions: Underline the complete subjects and double underline the simple subjects in each sentence below.

Example: <u>Most colleges</u> offer tutorial services to help students with their academic classes.

Most colleges in the United States offer some sort of academic assistance, such as tutorial services and writing centers. These services are often free. A tutor is someone who has already passed the class that the student needs help with, usually with a high grade. Also, tutors often are required to complete several hours of training in how to tutor others effectively. A second type of academic assistance is known as a writing center. At most writing centers, students can schedule appointments, or they can drop in without an appointment. Some writing centers will even help students with their papers by e-mail. Online writing labs, or OWLs, sponsored by various colleges and universities, can also provide valuable assistance with writing assignments. In addition, many colleges offer drop-in help with math, reading, biology, and other key subjects. The important thing to remember for all of these types of assistance is to arrive on time with a copy of your work, or at least a description of your assignment. You should have specific questions ready, and ask the tutor to help you learn from your mistakes.

1C: Recognizing Subjects and Verbs

Directions: In each sentence, underline the complete subject, and circle the simple subject. Double underline each verb, verb phrase, or compound verb.

Example: Your first job can teach you many skills that you will need later in life.

My first real job, at age 16, was as a stock clerk at the nearby TG&Y variety store. I had never worked in a business before, so the store manager's goal was to bring me up to speed on the "rules" of the retail world. The first rule was to arrive slightly early every day so that we could start right on time. The second rule of the store was not to sit down while counting stock or dusting shelves. Rules three and four prohibited gossip about the other employees and customers. The fifth rule was to volunteer for another job as soon as one job was finished. In addition to these five rules of retail work, the manager included many other valuable skills in my training. Stock rotation and customer assistance might not have been the most exciting skills to learn; however, everything about my experience at the TG&Y would help me in my later jobs.

1D: Recognizing Subjects and Verbs

Directions: In each sentence, underline the complete subject, and circle the simple subject. Double underline each verb, verb phrase, or compound verb.

Example: A wood-burning stove may improve the heating efficiency of your fireplace.

A stack of logs burning in a fireplace certainly gives a warm and cozy feeling, but that fireplace could actually be cooling your house and costing you hundreds of dollars a year in heating costs. The reason for this is that an open fireplace draws warm, heated air from the room, and then cold air leaks in around doors, windows, pipes, and wires. However, if you are not willing to give up the idea of a cozy evening in front of a blazing fire, there are several steps you can take to improve the heating efficiency of your fireplace. One solution is to install glass doors to reduce how much warm air is pulled up the chimney. Another possibility is to use an outdoor air supply, which completely eliminates the loss of warm house air. The third idea is to use a fireplace heater to recirculate the hot air, and the fourth option would be to install a fireback, a metal sheet that absorbs heat and radiates it into the room. Finally, some people decide to install a wood stove that fits into the fireplace and radiates even more heat into the room. Each of these options will keep you warmer and use less firewood, and you will enjoy your fireplace more than ever.

2A: Correcting Phrase Fragments and Subordinate Clause Fragments

Directions: Underline the fragments in the following passage. Then, on a separate piece of paper, revise the passage by correcting the fragments.

Example: Some people have trouble expressing their feelings. <u>And their needs.</u>

Corrected: *Some people have trouble expressing their feelings and their needs.*

Many colleges offer personal development classes. Which often include something called assertiveness training. Unfortunately, the term "assertive" is often misunderstood. Some people think that being assertive means the same thing. As being aggressive. However, assertiveness and aggressiveness are actually very different. A person who is aggressive tends to be argumentative. And forceful. An aggressive person often intimidates or offends people. Trying to force his or her opinions on others. On the other hand, when you are assertive. You stand up for your rights in a non-threatening manner. To be assertive, you should clearly state. What you want. It is important to speak up for yourself. And not let other people bully you into going along with their ideas. For example, do not agree to drive a friend to work every day. Or keep his pet rabbits for a month. Unless you really want to do these things. By learning to assert yourself without becoming aggressive. You will feel better about yourself. In addition, you will gain the respect of others.

2B: Correcting Fragments

Directions: Underline the fragments in the following passage. Remember to check for missing subjects or verbs, incomplete verb forms, phrase fragments, and subordinate clause fragments. Then, on a separate piece of paper, revise the passage by correcting the fragments.

Example: Although about 17% of Americans exercise more than an hour each day. Most of us get far less than the recommended minimum of 20 minutes of daily exercise.

Corrected: *Although about 17% of Americans exercise more than an hour each day, most of us get far less than the recommended minimum of 20 minutes of daily exercise.*

What does it mean? To be an average American? Many people don't like the idea of being average. Because they think "average" is a negative word. They associate "average" with getting C's in school instead of A's and B's. However, "average" as a statistical term just means. That you match up with most people. For instance, the average American stays indoors most of the time. Spending only 5% of the day outdoors. If you spend the majority of your time indoors, you are doing what the average American does. The average American still lives in the state where he or she was born. Spends about 2 1/2 hours online per day. And driving a car that is eight years old. In the last forty or fifty years, the lifestyle of the average American has changed. Forty or fifty years ago. Almost all families had only one wage earner, and mothers typically stayed home. The typical family no longer has a mother who does not work outside the home. And a father who is responsible for bringing home all of the income. Another change. Most American households more televisions than people.

2C: Correcting Fragments

Directions: Underline the fragments in the following passage. Remember to check for missing subjects or verbs, incomplete verb forms, phrase fragments, and subordinate clause fragments. Then, on a separate piece of paper, revise the passage by correcting the fragments.

Example: Because of their busy lifestyles. Adults find less personal time to spend with other adults. Than they did thirty or forty years ago.

Corrected: *Because of their busy lifestyles, adults find less personal time to spend with other adults than they did thirty or forty years ago.*

The average American's lifestyle today is a very busy one. How do busy parents still find time? To spend with their children? How do busy college students manage to work full-time or part-time? And still get good grades in their classes? One solution is multitasking. Or doing more than one thing at a time. We may make business calls and schedule appointments using our cell phones. While we are watching a sports event or waiting for a movie to start. We often hear people making personal calls. While they are shopping. Or waiting in line at the supermarket. Perhaps doing your homework. While watching television or listening to music. If you listen to audio books while you are driving. You may be able to complete some of your assignments. During your commute. You may sometimes meet with friends for lunch. And a study session at the same time. Although multitasking can help us accomplish more things in less time. We need to be careful. If we try to do too much, we may become easily distracted and unable to focus on a single important task.

3A: Combining Simple Sentences to Create Complex Sentences

Directions: Rewrite the following paragraph, using subordinating conjunctions and relative pronouns to create complex sentences where they are appropriate. You may choose to leave some sentences as they are.

Example: In Beni-Hassan, Egypt, archeologists discovered a cat cemetery. The cemetery contained 300,000 cat mummies.

Using Subordination: In Beni-Hassan, Egypt, archeologists discovered a cat cemetery *that contained 300,000 cat mummies.*

Dogs are said to be man's best friend. Cats are actually the most popular pets in the United States. Cats were originally valued for their pest control skills. They caught mice and rats in grain storage areas. People could store their surplus crops more securely. They didn't have to worry about rodents and other pests getting into the storage bins. In ancient Egypt, cats were revered. In fact, the Egyptian goddess of love had the head of a cat. The goddess's name was Bastet. Killing a cat in ancient Egypt was a crime. The crime was punishable by death. Ancient Romans also had high regard for cats. Cats were considered a symbol of liberty. During the Middle Ages in Europe, however, cats came to be associated with evil. Many cats were killed. They were thought to be representatives of witches and the devil. Unfortunately, there were few cats left to hunt and kill rats. The rats could spread the plague throughout Europe. Some people are still superstitious about cats. More than one third of all households in this country have at least one domesticated cat.

3B: Combining Simple Sentences to Create Compound Sentences

Directions: Rewrite the following paragraph, using coordinating conjunctions, conjunctive adverbs, or semicolons to create compound sentences where they are appropriate. You may choose to leave some sentences as they are.

Example: Washington is the only state named after a president. Many cities and counties are named after presidents.

Using Coordination: *Washington is the only state named after a president; **however**, many cities and counties are named after presidents.*

The state of Washington has a landscape that is full of contrasts. To the west, Washington is bordered by the Pacific Ocean. There are many large islands, waterways, and rivers. This area is famous for salmon and trout fishing. Near the coast, annual rainfall is as much as 180 inches in some places. There are thick, lush evergreen rain forests. The middle of the state consists of a high mountain range. These mountains have many tall, snow-covered peaks. Several peaks rise to more than 9,000 feet. Many people come to Washington to ski every year. Hikers, rock climbers, and mountain bikers enjoy the many recreational opportunities in these mountains. There are quite a few inactive volcanoes in this range. One volcano, Mount St. Helens, erupted in 1980. The western part of the state is very wet. East of the Cascade Mountains, there are dry, treeless plains. This area is very productive. Irrigation turns the dry land into rich farmland.

3C: Using Coordination and Subordination

Directions: Rewrite the following paragraph to emphasize ideas, to show connections among ideas, and to make the writing smooth. Change some of the simple sentences to compound and complex sentences. You may choose to leave some sentences as they are.

Example: French soccer star Thierry Henry was once insulted with racial slurs by a professional coach. He has led the fight to eliminate racism in European soccer.

Correction: *French soccer star Thierry Henry, **who** was once insulted with racial slurs by a professional coach, has led the fight to eliminate racism in European soccer.*

Some celebrities use their power and influence to help people around the world. These people suffer from poverty, disease, or violence. They may lack opportunities for education. Near Johannesburg, South Africa, Oprah Winfrey established The Oprah Winfrey Leadership Academy for Girls. This academy helps young women in grades 7-12 achieve their full potential through education. It will make a real difference in the future for South African women. Actor George Clooney made his first trip to Darfur in 2006. He has become a spokesperson for raising awareness about the suffering of people in Darfur. He has become an advocate for taking action against the genocide there. Another actor, Michael J. Fox, was diagnosed with Parkinson's disease in 1991. He was only 30 years old. He has become a leading activist in the fight to find a cure for Parkinson's. He speaks publicly on behalf of others. They cannot speak for themselves. They might be cured by stem-cell treatments.

4A: Recognizing Comma Splices and Run-ons

Directions: The following paragraph contains several comma splices and run-on sentences. Put an * in front of any comma splice or run-on, and insert a / where a period or sentence connector is needed.

Example: *Computers have become a part of our daily lives,/ we rely on them for education, business, and entertainment.

During the last few years, more and more people have come to rely on computers the number of Internet users is increasing every day. By 2007, there were more than 237 million Internet users in North America. Some people use the Internet for business or educational purposes, others use it mainly for entertainment. Entertainment possibilities include meeting people in chat rooms, playing games online, and downloading pictures of your favorite sports figures or movie stars. Another possibility is cyber-dating, keep in mind, however, that meeting a "cyber-date" in real life could be dangerous. People you meet online may not always tell the truth about themselves. For example, someone who claims to be twenty-five may actually turn out to be fifteen or forty-five unethical individuals may also lie about other things, such as their job, their physical appearance, or their marital status. Although you may be lucky enough to get acquainted online with people who become lifelong friends, it is important to be cautious.

4B: Correcting Comma Splices and Run-ons

Directions: First, identify comma splices and run-ons in the following passage by putting an * in front of each one. Then correct the comma splices and run-ons by adding a coordinating conjunction, a subordinating conjunction, a relative connector, a conjunctive adverb, a semicolon, or a period. In some cases, more than one solution is possible.

Example: *Commercials are big business, large companies will pay millions of dollars to place their ads on highly rated television programs.

Corrected: *Commercials are big business; large companies will pay millions of dollars to place their ads on highly rated television programs.*

A cute, friendly gecko tries to persuade us to buy a certain brand of insurance, a quacking duck encourages us to choose a different company. Talking sheep have an opinion about which mattress will help us sleep soundly, happy cows want us to believe that California cheese is the best. Television commercials use any techniques they can to capture viewers' attention their goal is to persuade consumers to buy their products. Celebrities endorse a variety of items, from sports drinks to medicines to credit cards. Many commercials appeal to younger viewers they are the prime target of a large number of advertisers. Enthusiastic singers and dancers try to persuade young people to buy clothes at certain stores, if they wear these clothes they will be part of the popular "in crowd." Although teenagers don't have unlimited funds, they have a great deal of influence on household spending, advertisers hope they will form lifetime shopping habits. The same brands that they buy and use as teenagers are likely to remain their favorite brands ten or twenty years from now.

4C: Correcting Comma Splices and Run-ons

Directions: First, identify comma splices and run-ons in the following passage by putting an * in front of each one. Then correct the comma splices and run-ons by adding a coordinating conjunction, a subordinating conjunction, a relative connector, a conjunctive adverb, a semicolon, or a period. In some cases, more than one solution is possible.

Example: *The Amazon River was named after a group of powerful female warriors, they lived in rain forests of the Amazon River Basin.

Corrected: *The Amazon River was named after a group of powerful female warriors **who** lived in rain forests of the Amazon River Basin.*

The Amazon River in South America is the second longest river in the world, the only river that is longer is the Nile in Africa. However, the Amazon carries a greater volume of water than any other river, it has more tributaries, or smaller rivers that feed into it. The Amazon begins at Lake Lauricocha in the Andes Mountains of Peru several other rivers join it to become part of the Amazon as it flows eastward, finally emptying into the Atlantic Ocean. Before reaching the ocean off the eastern coast of Brazil, the Amazon has traveled a total length of more than 4,000 miles. The velocity of the river averages about 1.5 miles per hour eight trillion gallons of water per day are emptied into the Atlantic by the mighty Amazon. More than three hundred species of mammals make their homes in the Amazon rain forest, as well as thousands of species of fish, amphibians, reptiles, birds, and insects. Piranhas, which are found in parts of the river, can quickly kill and eat the flesh of a person, toucans do not live in the wild anywhere except the Amazon area, they are birds with huge beaks. Freshwater dolphins also live in parts of the river, they are called botos or pink dolphins.

4D: Correcting Comma Splices and Run-ons

Directions: First, identify comma splices and run-ons in the following passage by putting an * in front of each one. Then correct the comma splices and run-ons by adding a coordinating conjunction, a subordinating conjunction, a relative connector, a conjunctive adverb, a semicolon, or a period. In some cases, more than one solution is possible.

Example: *Khaled Hosseini is probably the most well-known Afghan in the world his books have not been published in Afghanistan.

Corrected: *Khaled Hosseini is probably the most well-known Afghan in the world, but his books have not been published in Afghanistan.*

Khaled Hosseini now lives in San Jose, California, he writes about his native country of Afghanistan. His first novel, *The Kite Runner*, almost instantly became a major bestseller, with more than four million copies sold in the first three years. The story begins with two young boys in 1970s Afghanistan, they have grown up together and are very close, Amir has a much higher status because ethnically he is a Pashtun, Amir's loyal friend Hassan is a Hazara and a family servant. A shocking event tears their friendship apart, from then on Amir carries the guilt of not defending or helping his friend. Years later, when Amir is living in the United States as part of the Afghan-American community, a call from an old family friend draws him back to Afghanistan in search of redemption. In 2007 *The Kite Runner* was adapted into a movie, it was filmed just across Afghanistan's border in and near Kashgar, China. Many of the actors are Afghans, including the boys, much of the dialogue is in the Dari language of Afghanistan. In addition to telling a story of complex relationships, loyalty, and redemption, the film raises awareness about conditions in Afghanistan.

14

5A: Basic Subject-Verb Agreement

Directions: The following paragraph contains a number of errors in subject-verb agreement with special subjects, including collective subjects, compound subjects, indefinite pronouns, and others. Cross out the errors and write the correct verb form above the line.

Example:
Movie ratings ~~gives~~ *give* us some guidelines about whether violence or adult
scenes ~~is~~ *are* featured in a certain movie.

People goes to the movies to be entertained, but their ideas about good entertainment varies. Some viewers prefer to laugh, to enjoy happy endings, and to feel good when they leaves the movie theater. Others enjoys action and adventure movies, even if there is violent scenes where someone get killed or injured and there are lots of blood. Apparently, not everyone experience on-screen violence in the same way. Some are haunted by scenes of maimed bodies or bloody crime scenes, but those kinds of scenes does not bother everyone. Some of us blocks out gruesome scenes by closing our eyes. Reminding ourselves that the scenes is not real may also help. Horror movies takes gruesome scenes even further. Characters may narrowly escape monsters, evil spirits, or beings from the underworld. Terror and suspense is sometimes overwhelming. Perhaps some moviegoers enjoys being frightened, or maybe they has already seen so much violence that they are no longer affected by it. Indeed, today's video games, computer simulations, and horrifying movies exposes young people to an extraordinary amount of violence.

5B: Maintaining Agreement with Indefinite Pronouns, Collective Nouns, and Compound Subjects

Directions: Correct all errors in subject-verb agreement. Most of the agreement errors involve indefinite pronouns, collective nouns, or compound subjects. For each error, draw a line through the incorrect verb, and write the correct form above the line.

Example:
> *helps*
> A supportive group to belong to ~~help~~ a person feel secure.

Nobody want to be a misfit. Everyone need to feel accepted and valued by others. Without that kind of group acceptance, one is likely to lead a lonely, isolated life. A group offer a sense of security and belonging to all its members. Family or friends provides an extremely important group identity for most people. For example, sisters, brothers, and cousins all feels a sense of belonging to the same family and generally remains loyal to the family unit. In return, the family also give them something. A set of values, acceptance, and unconditional love are a few of the most important benefits. Many people is members of several different groups in addition to their family. A sports team offer many of the same rewards, and so do a club or a Scout troop. Unfortunately, some young people today find their group identity in a gang. To them, a gang become almost like a family. Although none of us can choose the family that we are born into, all of us needs to choose our other group memberships wisely.

5C: Correcting Subject-Verb Agreement Errors

Directions: Correct all errors in subject-verb agreement. Draw a line through the incorrect verb, and write the correct form above the line.

Example:
                                  are
Both men and women ~~is~~ genetically programmed to search for a mate.

Members of a species has to mate and produce offspring, or the species will not continue. From a biological perspective, that explain why young adults of both sexes searches for an appropriate mate. To help with this search, various "mating rituals" encourage members of the opposite sex to spend time getting acquainted with a potential mate before they makes a commitment. For many young people, dances, parties, sports, and other social events offer opportunities to get to know members of the opposite sex. If you watches people interacting at a social event, you can tell who are interested in someone else by their conversation and their body language. Subtle gestures like raising eyebrows, tilting the head, standing a certain way, or other nonverbal cues indicates a person is flirting. Most people interprets these unspoken signals as signs of interest without even thinking about it. However, the motivations behind our dating, mating, and marrying choices is complex. When someone is looking for romance, he or she are actually looking for a compatible combination of physiological and neurochemical factors, according to scientists. Sounds, smells, hormones, and brain chemistry all plays a role in our choices.

6A: Using *Will* to Show Future Time

Directions: In the following paragraph, cross out some of the present tense verbs and show future time using *will* wherever it is appropriate.

Example:

                            will be

                          Less oil ~~is~~ produced in the future.

     Futurist.com is a Web site and blog that is dedicated to helping predict the future and prepare for it. One of its articles talks about "ticking time bombs" that cause problems in the future. For example, oil demand increases because of the growing economies of countries like India and China, but the amount of oil produced diminishes after reaching a peak sometime around the year 2015. Another example is that the middle class experiences more problems because energy and commodity prices increase, but wages probably do not keep up with inflation. The other five ticking time bombs include global warming, illegal immigration, the possibility of a giant asteroid strike, the inability of the government to pay off its debts, and a worldwide epidemic. While we don't know which of these events occurs in our lifetimes, *Futurist.com* continues to provide information on all of these possible scenarios. Take time out of your busy day to check out this interesting Web site—you aren't sorry that you did.

6B: Using the Past Tense

Directions: In the following paragraph, change the present tense verbs to the past tense.

worked
Example: Six people ~~work~~ several hours to clean up after the picnic.

To get ready for the our church's big potluck picnic, we reserve the picnic area at the park three months in advance. At 11:00 on the day of the picnic, we pull into the park, park the car, and unload the canopy, chairs, and food that we prepare that morning. Many of our friends and their families arrive soon afterward. The first thing we do is to visit with each other, and some of the children and their fathers are throwing a football back and forth. After the prayer, we enter the line and help ourselves to some of the many dishes that people have prepared, which include some of my favorite foods: fried chicken, macaroni, beans, watermelon, brownies, grapes, and chocolate chip cookies. After we eat and visit with some friends, the younger children enjoy snow cones, and later, jump on the trampoline. The older children play softball, and the parents mostly just talk and joke and share a relaxing afternoon together. As usual, the last thing before we leave to go home is to pack everything up into pickups, vans, and cars. Then we look around to see if the area is clean and head for home, already looking forward to next year's picnic.

6C: Using the Perfect Tenses

Directions: In the following paragraph, some of the present tense verbs are underlined. Change these present tense verbs to the present perfect, past perfect, or future perfect forms, as appropriate.

Example: Adding compost to the soil this year ~~improves~~ **_has improved_** it a lot.

Before last March, it <u>is</u> several years since I <u>plant</u> a vegetable garden. For several years before that, I was too busy, or too disorganized, to plant a garden. This year, I <u>plant</u> only squash and tomatoes so far, but the results already <u>impress</u> me. The squash <u>is</u> ready for several weeks already, and we <u>pick</u> a lot of squash. I planted the tomatoes late this year, so they are not ripe yet. By next month, we <u>savor</u> our first ripe, homegrown tomatoes, and we are very much looking forward to that wonderful, sweet-tart flavor. In fall I will look at the newest online seed catalogs, such as Renee's Garden Seeds at <u>www.reneesgarden.com</u>, and by December I hope that I <u>order</u> most of the seeds for next year's garden. I recommend gardening to everyone, even if you only have room for one cherry tomato plant. If you never <u>garden</u> before, you might be surprised at how satisfying it is to grow your own vegetables.

7A: Using Irregular Verbs Correctly

Directions: Cross out each verb in parentheses, and write in the correct past tense form or past participle form, as appropriate. Include a helping verb if necessary.

Example:
became
The radio (become) a popular form of family entertainment in the 1920s.

Many authors (write) about the 1920s, including F. Scott Fitzgerald. Although Fitzgerald's book *The Great Gatsby* (be) not popular when it was first published in 1925, in recent years many thousands of college students (read) it. Some people say that they (know) nothing about the 1920s before reading *The Great Gatsby*. However, afterward, they (understand) something about the lavish and often carefree lifestyle of the rich during that era. At the beginning of the decade, in 1920, the 18th Amendment (go) into effect, establishing Prohibition nationwide. This (mean) that anyone who produced or (sell) alcoholic beverages was breaking the law. Organized crime (take) advantage of the situation, and bootleggers (make) alcohol available to those who could afford it. The 1920s (become) known as "the Roaring Twenties." Many people (be) in a free-spirited mood after the end of "The Great War," World War I, and (seek) thrills or excitement in various ways. In 1927, Charles Lindbergh (make) history when he (fly) across the Atlantic in 33 hours, and people (see) him as a hero. Another popular hero who (rise) to fame in the 1920s was Babe Ruth, baseball's "Sultan of Swat."

7B: Correcting Errors with *Can / Could, Will / Would*, and Forms of *to Be*

Directions: Correct errors in the use of *can* and *could, will* and *would*, and the forms of the verb *to be*. Cross out the incorrect forms and write the correct forms above the line.

Example: *can*
                  Nowadays we ~~could~~ watch movies in theaters, rent them, see them on network television, buy them on DVDs, or even download them from the Internet.

Life is so different now than it been at the beginning of the twentieth century that we could hardly imagine how people lived then. For example, now we can see all the latest movies, watch television, or listen to the radio whenever we want to. Movies was popular in the early 1900s also, but they were very different from the modern movies that we could watch today. The technology to add sound be not in existence until the 1920s. Viewers of early movies will read the dialogue in "titles," or lines of print on the screen. Unlike movies, radio and television was not in existence yet in 1900. Although the first radio communication signal had been sent in 1895 by an Italian inventor named Marconi, the radio as we know it had not yet being invented. Ship-to-shore radio is operational before there was any radio stations that can broadcast programs, and in fact, many survivors of the *Titanic* probably will have died in 1912 without radio communication. The first commercial radio station probably been WWJ, in Detroit, Michigan. It was not until the 1920s that the average person can enjoy comedies, dramas, music, and soap operas on the radio, and several decades later before they can watch television every day.

7C: Correcting Errors with Irregular Verbs

Directions: Correct all errors with verbs in the following passage. Cross out the incorrect forms and write the correct forms above the line.

Example: *grew*
By 1945, World War II victory gardens ~~growed~~ 40% of the fruits and vegetables consumed in the United States.

Victory gardens is plots of land where ordinary people growed their own vegetables, herbs, and fruits to contribute to the war effort during World War II. Due to the need to supply the U.S. Army and British soldiers with canned food, the United States government maked victory gardens (also called "war gardens") an important part of the war effort in World War II. They come up with slogans like "Plant more in '44" to encourage citizens to did whatever they can to help. These gardens was located in back yards, parks, vacant lots, roofs of apartment buildings, and basically anywhere people find room to put in a few vegetables. In addition to fresh vegetables, they produced food for home canning for use during the non-growing season. When the soldiers come home after the war was over, many people stopped growning vegetables, and the victory gardens begun to disappear. The only public victory gardens still in existence today was Fenway Victory Gardens in Boston, Massachusetts, but most of them now grew flowers instead of vegetables. When times are difficult financially, growing your own vegetables can be a way to kept from spending so much money.

8A: Using Passive Voice

Directions: Rewrite the paragraph below, changing the underlined passive voice constructions to the active voice. Reword the sentences as necessary.

Example: An officer told Elena that ~~her car could not be located by the police~~.
                                            the police could not locate her car.

I learned a hard lesson during my early adult years when my 1969 Camaro with the flames on the sides was stolen. When <u>the decision was made</u> to sell the car, I took my precious baby to a local car lot, but <u>I was offered only a very low price by the manager</u>. Then <u>I was told by the manager</u> that <u>a better price for the car could be gotten</u> at an auction in a nearby big city, and that if I signed the pink slip, <u>the car could be sold</u> by him at the auction. I signed the pink slip, but I never saw my car again, and <u>no money was ever received</u>. After <u>$1200.00 was paid</u> to a lawyer, I eventually learned for sure that <u>my car had been stolen by the manager</u> and could not be recovered because it could not be found and he had no assets to pay for it with. Even today, I sometimes think of that car with a twinge of regret, and I wish that the police could have recovered my car and returned it to me. Needless to say, <u>a lesson was learned</u> that I will never forget.

8B: Using Passive Voice

Directions: Rewrite the paragraph below, changing the underlined passive voice constructions to the active voice. Reword the sentences as necessary.

Example:

Gene Autry wrote the popular Western song "Back in the Saddle Again."

The popular Western song "Back in the Saddle Again" ~~was written by Gene Autry.~~

In the early days of television, cowboys of the Old West <u>were featured</u> in many popular shows. The transition from radio to television <u>was</u> successfully <u>made</u> by many cowboy programs. For example, "The Gene Autry Show" <u>had been listened to</u> on the radio by millions of fans, who then became part of the show's television audience. Gene Autry <u>was known</u> by many as "The Singing Cowboy," and several Western movies <u>had been made</u> by him in the 1930s and 1940s. He starred in his first movie, "In Old Santa Fe," in 1934. During World War II, airplanes <u>were flown</u> by Autry as an officer in the Army Air Corps. Because of his interest in flying, his ranch in Oklahoma <u>was named</u> the Flying A by him. The Flying A Rodeo Company <u>was</u> also <u>owned</u> by Autry. In Gene Autry's lifetime, more than 600 recordings <u>were made</u> by him, and more than 200 songs <u>were written</u> by him, including "Back in the Saddle Again," one of the most well-known Western songs of the twentieth century. In 1949, the first recording of "Rudolph the Red-Nosed Reindeer" <u>was made</u> by him after the opportunity <u>had been turned down</u> by several other singers. With more than 30 million copies sold, "Rudolph the Red-Nosed Reindeer" is still the second top-selling single of all time.

8C: Using Progressive Tenses

Directions: Choose an appropriate progressive tense of each underlined verb and write it above that verb.

Example:
> ***had been looking***
> We <u>had looked</u> forward to that vacation for months.

The summer after my high school graduation, two friends and I left San Diego and went on a driving trip around California, visiting Yosemite, the Gold Country, San Francisco, Disneyland, and several other places. As we <u>traveled</u> north on Interstate 15, we talked about all the things we would miss about high school, as well as what we <u>expected</u> from our future lives. "By the year 2000, I <u>hope</u> to be a millionaire," announced one of my friends. "You <u>will probably still work</u> at the hamburger store," joked my other friend. "No way," I broke in. "He <u>has planned</u> his get-rich strategy in detail for over a year now. He'll be a millionaire for sure." While we <u>drove</u>, we laughed, joked, and discussed what we wanted to see at each destination. Being out on the road with no real responsibilities felt great because all three of us <u>had worked</u> many hours per week while we were in high school, and we had college and jobs lined up ahead of us as well. Even though the vacation <u>passed</u> by too quickly, we enjoyed it while we could.

8D: Maintaining Consistency in Tense

Directions: There are many inconsistencies in verb tense in the paragraph below. Cross out each error, and write the correct verb form above it.

Example:
>   *insisted*
> While we were visiting Chinatown in San Francisco, my uncle Burt ~~insists~~ on taking us to an Italian restaurant.

San Francisco is one of the highlights of our driving trip around California. It was a real metropolis, with many activities going on and a lot of interesting things to see. The first day, we rode on the cable cars, climb Nob Hill to see Coit Tower, drive down twisty Lombard Street on Russian Hill, and buy freshly-steamed crabs and fresh-baked sourdough bread for a picnic dinner in Golden Gate Park. The next day we travel over the Golden Gate Bridge and visited cool and shady Muir Woods with its giant redwood trees, and when we come back we shop for chocolate and souvenirs at Ghirardelli Square and Pier 39. Our third day in the city, we see Little Japan and ate sitting on the floor at a real Japanese restaurant. On the last day, we go to Chinatown, my favorite part of San Francisco, where we saw older Chinese gentlemen reading the newspapers that had been posted in shop windows for that purpose. We notice that they read the Chinese characters from top to bottom, as they gradually bend lower and lower until they come to the bottom of each column, and then straighten up again to read the next line. Next time I go to San Francisco, I want to see Alcatraz and the museums in Golden Gate Park.

9A: Using Personal Pronouns Correctly

Directions: Most sentences in the following paragraph contain one or more errors in personal pronoun use. Cross out the incorrect pronouns, and write the correct forms above them.

Example: *their*
The boys enjoyed riding ~~they're~~ bikes after school.

It seems like only yesterday that me and my friend Billy were starting first grade together at Parkview Elementary School. Trouble always seemed to follow him and I when we were kids. Taking the long way home through the canyon was a big temptation for us, and us usually gave in to temptation. Hi's mother never got mad at he for coming home late, but mines parents did. When Billy and me were a little older, we always had to do ours homework right away. "If its not done, yous can't go out and play," my mom would tell I. Sometimes she would ask my to do other important jobs too, like giving the cats there food or taking the dog for a walk on it's leash. If Billy finished his' work first, he would ride he's bike over to ours house and wait for me. Him was very polite and respectful to my mother, so she always thought him was a good kid. She had no idea how much mischief the two of ours could get into! "Look at this floor," she would say. "Who got him so dirty?" Me and him would give them a big smile and try to look innocent, as if we hadn't done them. Billy and me are in college now, but we are still friends. Just between you and I, we still get into trouble once in a while.

9B: Using Indefinite Pronouns and Verbs Correctly

Directions: There are several errors involving indefinite pronouns in the paragraph below. Cross out each incorrect pronoun or verb form, and write the corrected form on the line above.

Example:
          are
Many brides ~~is~~ choosing Bob Carlisle's *Butterfly Kisses* for the first dance with their fathers, at their wedding receptions.

Most fathers is shocked to see his daughters grow up. Watching a child mature is a difficult passage in life, and its effects are deep. One popular song, Bob Carlisle's *Butterfly Kisses*, sets this theme to music and expresses what many dads feels as each one see his daughter going to kindergarten for the first time, then high school, often college, and in many cases, getting married. Few of the other fathers that I know wants to talk about this topic because it is too emotional. The others prefers to ignore it, or suffer in silence, as they see their role in their daughters' lives changing. None of the fathers that I know has openly acknowledged the bittersweet emotions that come as a result of moving from their traditional role of protector to that of caring bystander, even though most of us has done our best to equip them to be successful and independent adults. Everyone say that fathers aren't as emotional as mothers, but as the father of four daughters, I know that this isn't true, even if we sometimes wish it were. As fathers, we hope that each one of our daughters feel confident enough to make her own way in life, but we also hope that our daughters will still love us even when they no longer needs us as they did when they were young.

9C: Using Nouns and Pronouns Correctly

Directions: The following sentences contain errors in the use and spelling of nouns and pronouns. Cross out the errors and write the corrections above. Make sure subject nouns agree with their verbs. Finally, make sure the pronoun case is correct.

Example:
> *your*
> Credit card debt can make ~~you're~~ life miserable.

Credit cards can be very enticing to you and I, but they might not be aware of the true cost and risks of credit cards. It's hard for anyone to resist the advertisements that announce "Live richly," "Make life rewarding," and "It pays to Discover," but credit cards make it so easy to buy things that someone might forget you're spending actual money, and he can get in over his head. People who gets carried away and buy things impulsively, without planning ahead, can end up in real trouble when it comes time to pay back what she owes—with interest! In addition to late fees and higher interest rates, a bad credit rating might keep them from getting a high-level job or even renting the house or apartment of your choice. Perhaps the worst things about credit cards is that if we get behind in your payments, some collections agencies will call several times a day and threaten legal action. Consumers do have certain rights and protections, however, and the popular show <u>Frontline</u> on PBS has an Internet site with links to many useful information about credit cards at <u>http://www.pbs.org/wgbh/pages/frontline/shows/credit/</u>. The best advice is probably to keep only one or two cards, and to do her best to pay off her balance when it comes.

10A: Using Adjectives and Adverbs Correctly

Directions: Correct all errors in the use of adjectives and adverbs. Draw a line through the error, and write the correct form above the line.

Example: Sheila and Greg thought Introduction to Philosophy was one of the ~~bestest~~ *best* classes they had ever taken.

The atmosphere in the philosophy classroom was tensely as the students waited anxiously for their new professor to arrive. Dr. Roland Wolff, whose lectures were always real interesting and whose tests were always easily, had retired very sudden in the middle of the semester. Rumor had it that the day after he retired, he had taken off quick for a secret destination in the South Pacific, where he planned to live quietly and comfortable for the rest of his life. He had always lived the most privatest life of any professor on campus, so it was not real strange or remarkably that he had gone off by himself. However, he would be greatly missed. None of the students knew anything about Dr. Quoyle, who had agreed to take over Dr. Wolff's classes on shortest notice. When his largest frame appeared in the doorway, they couldn't help but stare. Dr. Quoyle was a very tallest man with red hair and the most biggest chin they had ever seen. However, after he announced that he was going to cut two books from the reading list, they began to feel more better. Maybe they would like Dr. Quoyle after all.

10B: Correcting Double Negatives

Directions: Correct the double negatives in the following paragraph. Draw a line through words that need to be changed and write your revision above the line.

Example: Your auto insurance rates will be lower if you never have *~~no~~* **any** accidents.

For the first six months after getting her driver's license, Taiko didn't get into no accidents at all. That all changed her first week of community college. The first accident happened when she was backing out of the driveway. Her foot slipped onto the gas pedal instead of the brake, and she backed into another car. She was shaken up quite a bit and didn't know nothing about what to do or who to call, so we helped her calm down and told her that an accident can happen to anybody. The second accident happened when two other cars ran into each other, then suddenly stopped right in front of her. She didn't have not enough time to stop, and gently bumped into the car in front of her. She didn't hardly bump it at all, but the driver got out and yelled at her, even though there wasn't no damage to neither car. Her third bad experience didn't never really happen—it was a nightmare about losing control while driving, then getting out of the car and standing in the rain watching it burn. Now Taiko is worried about her insurance rates going up, but the most important things are that she is safe, that nobody wasn't injured, and that she hasn't never given up on driving in spite of her two accidents and one bad dream. She hopes that she won't have no more accidents for a long, long time.

10C: Correcting Errors with Modifiers

Directions: Correct all errors involving incorrect forms of adjectives or adverbs and misplaced or dangling *-ing* modifiers. Cross out each error and write the correct form or correct phrase above the line. In some cases, you may need to rewrite an entire sentence or clause.

Example:

> ***Riding my bicycle in a remote area, I saw a rattlesnake.***
> ~~I saw a rattlesnake riding my bicycle~~ in a remote area.

Before the young campers arrived, the campground seemed quietly and peacefully. As a real new camp counselor, I was eager to look around the area, so I started to explore. I saw ground squirrels and lizards hiking along the trails. The most biggest crow that I had ever seen scolded me loudly sitting in a tree. Jumping out of the lake, I saw several fish, and a few wild ducks and loons were swimming slow and graceful. I imagined the real enthusiastic youngsters paddling canoes wearing orange life vests. Then, blowing across the water, I noticed the wind, and hugely dark clouds appeared on the other side of the lake racing across the sky. Bright flashes of lightning were followed by distantly sounds of thunder. Running back toward the campground, the approaching storm was starting to frighten me bad. Soon rain started coming down hard, and my clothes were completely soaked. Finally, approaching one of the cabins, I decided to go inside and take shelter from the storm that had begun so quick. Laughing and talking with each other, I found some of the other camp counselors already inside the cabin. Joining them, I began to relax and enjoy the rainy weather.

11A: Correcting Errors in Agreement with Indefinite Pronouns

Directions: Cross out each error, and then write the correction above it. Change the verb and/or other words if necessary. More than one correct answer may be possible.

Example: Many students have different goals for ~~his or her~~ *their* college experience.

Or: ***Each student has a different goal*** ~~Many students have~~ ~~different goals~~ for his or her college experience.

In today's higher education, not every college student fits the stereotypical image of the full-time scholar who is determined to receive their traditional four-year degree in the shortest time possible. While many college students still have a degree as his or her goal, others are taking shorter courses of study to prepare themselves for a career. In addition, someone who has a full-time job may register for classes in math, writing, or their chosen field in order to improve the chances of getting a promotion. Finally, many college classes have a few students who are studying for personal or family reasons, such as sheer love of learning, mastering a foreign language for travel, or improving their basic skills in order to help his or her children with their homework. All of these students have their own goals and reasons to study in college, and each college should give him the welcome he deserves. Everyone who is willing to study hard in college deserves our full support and encouragement, no matter what their goals are.

11B: Correcting Unclear or Ambiguous Pronoun References

Directions: Cross out each unclear or ambiguous pronoun reference, and then write a correction above it. Change the verb if necessary. More than one correct answer may be possible.

Example: The local community college offers many of ~~their~~ *its* courses online.

Many colleges offer programs for non-traditional students, and in recent years, a number of students have taken advantage of them. At many colleges, evening and weekend academic programs provide an opportunity for those who cannot attend school Monday through Friday during the day because of their full-time jobs or family responsibilities. Online courses are also becoming more and more popular. This enables people who live at a considerable distance from any college or university to enroll in them, or someone with a disability may prefer taking them online. At some colleges, an older or "re-entry" student may be able to see a special counselor if she needs information about college programs and resources. A large number of colleges now have special resource centers for returning female students. They can help with arrangements for financial aid, orientation to the college, childcare, career choices, and other issues that are important to them. Extra tutoring may also be available to students who need help with a content class or basic writing or math skills. It can mean the difference between getting a good grade in a class or dropping out. Investigating all the resources that are available can make it easier.

Directions: Proofread the following paragraph for problems with pronoun-antecedent agreement and sexist language. Make any necessary changes by crossing out the incorrect word and writing a more effective choice above it. More than one correct answer may be possible.

Example: *Women* ~~A woman~~ now *have* ~~has~~ a greater variety of career choices than they used to.

Fifty years ago, career choices for women were limited. She could choose to be a teacher, a nurse, a secretary, or a homemaker. At that time, parents were likely to disapprove if she made any other choice, so it would be difficult. Sons could dream of being airline pilots, policemen, doctors, or business executives if he wanted to, but daughters could not. Most young women chose careers that conformed to traditional gender roles, but not everyone did it. For example, a female friend of mine was one of the first women to major in engineering at Northwestern University. One of my aunts chose architecture as their field and found that all of the other students in their classes were male. In any predominately male program, a woman had to try harder to prove themselves. Fortunately, traditional gender roles have changed over the years. Now a woman can become an FBI agent, a firefighter, a research chemist, or a computer programmer if they want to. In fact, more women all the time are choosing careers that used to be reserved almost exclusively for a man. Both college applications and job applications are generally reviewed without regard to the applicant's gender, so with hard work anyone can obtain the job that he wants.

12A: Using Parallel Words in a Series

Directions: Several sentences in the following paragraph contain errors in parallelism. Cross out the errors, and write the correct version above the faulty one, if necessary.

Example: Our college offers classes in swimming, running, soccer, baseball, and ~~to learn~~ racquetball.

Regular exercise is valuable to reduce stress, increase general health, and extending a person's lifespan. More specifically, exercise improves cardio-respiratory fitness, muscular strength, muscular endurance, flexibility, and your body composition becomes healthier. Research has shown that people who exercise regularly are less likely to suffer from stress, depression, or even problems in a relationship. Whether you choose to lift weights, participate in a physical education class, take up a martial art, join a team, or just walking or running regularly, exercise can give you a happier life. Other options for the more adventurous include kayaking, mountain biking, surfing, to snowboard, or a mountain climb. Finally, extreme options include ice climbing, downhill mountain bike racing, and freestyle ski jumping. Whichever option you choose, be sure to begin gradually and working up to more strenuous levels over time, or you may run the risk of injury.

12B: Using Parallel Structure with Phrases

Directions: Several sentences in the following paragraph contain errors in parallelism. Cross out the errors, and write the correct version above the faulty one, if necessary.

Example: Their family vacation in Hawaii included snorkeling in the bay, hiking into an

playing
extinct volcano, and ~~they played~~ golf on a beautiful course.

Many interesting recreational activities such as nature walks, group bicycle rides, stargazing, or going to a lecture on art and history are available in most communities, but they are not always well-advertised or you can't find them easily. One good source of information is the local newspaper. One day per week, many local newspapers offer a column on "What's Happening" at area galleries, museums, parks, and from sports facilities. Another rich source of information on local events is the Internet. Local sites such as "SDReader.com" (for San Diego) or "gophila.com" (for Philadelphia) carry a wealth of information on regional events and activities, and if you have America Online, to click on the "Local" channel. These recreational events can provide you with the opportunity of meeting new people and the chance to participate in interesting and fun activities.

12C: Maintaining Parallelism

Directions: Check the sentences in the following paragraph for errors in parallelism. Cross out each incorrect form, and write your correction in the space above.

Example: In addition to financial aid, many college scholarships are available for academic achievement, sports, music, specific majors, gender or ethnicity,

        membership in a particular organization

        ~~if you are a member of a particular organization~~, and many other reasons.

According to the College Board, there is nearly three billion dollars of scholarship aid available to college students and who want to go to college. Applying for these scholarships involves the following steps. First, find out about the scholarships through free online services such as Scholarship Search, Fastweb, Scholarship Research Network Express, and go to Wiredscholar. Next, choose the scholarships that seem to fit you and matching your interests and situation. After that, make a schedule to apply for one scholarship every week. It won't take long for you to get pretty good at filling out the applications and to write the personal narratives that need to be included with your application. Another important part of the application process is to ask for letters of recommendation. Remember to allow enough time for your letters to come in and not at the last minute. Being polite and to consider the schedule of the people you ask is a very important part of the process. If you follow these steps and don't forget to thank the people who help you, you may end up with your own small part of that three billion dollars.

13A: Correct Spelling of Words with Suffixes

Directions: Check for correct spelling in words ending with the suffixes *-able, -al, -ed, -ful, -ing, -ive, -ly, -ment,* and *-tion*. Cross out each incorrect form, and write the correct version above it.

Example:

                                                     graduated

It is possible for some students who have never ~~graduateed~~ from high school

    successfully

to ~~successfuly~~ attend college.

A college educateion is more expenseive now than ever before, but a little resourcefullnes in researching financial aid can make it more afforddable. While some occupations require a special talent or practical experience, statistics show that students who have graduatted from college are earnning, on average, much more than students who have only a high school diploma. Even takeing a few college courses can increase your earnings, but college is expenseive. The average cost for a year of college is over $6500, including educationall expenses and room and board. Private colleges cost much more, but they also offer more financeial aid; in fact, at many colleges, almost every student receives at least some financial aid, whether in the form of scholarships, loans, grants, or work/study jobs. If you are hopeing or planing to attend college, a careful investigashun of sources of help at a local library or on the Internet may realy pay off. Finaly, use good judgment in your financial arrangments. If you pay income taxes, you can even get a tax credit for part of your costs, and you can save money by liveing at home and attendding a nearby college.

13B: Using Commonly Confused and Commonly Misspelled Words

Directions: Check for correct spelling and usage in the following paragraph. Cross out each incorrect form, and write the correct version above it.

Example:

                advise   *exceeds*

Experts ~~advice~~ not taking on a debt that ~~excedes~~ your ability to repay.

A morgage is a kind of loan used to purchase real estate, such as a house or condominium. Most morgages must be paid off over a period of 15 to 40 years, and if the homebuyer stops paying, the agency or individual whom lent the money can take the house and sell it in order to pay off the remaining debt. Each time a payment is made, part of the money is credited to interest and the rest is credited to the principle, which is the original amount of money that was borrowed. There are many financial advantages to buying a home instead of renting, and at least too disadvantages. One advantage is that when interest rates are low, buyers can sometimes buy a property for fewer then it would cost to rent a similar property, and its possible to lock in a fixed payment that will never go up in the future. In addition, the U.S. government generaly permits morgage borrowers to deduct the interest they pay on their home loan from their income taxes. On the negative side, homeowners must pay state and local property taxes and all the costs to maintane and repair their homes. If your in the market for a home, a good stragety is to get good advise before you sign any papers, and be sure to shop around for the best interest rates and the lowest loan fees. If you now the basic facts about a morgage, you will enjoy the benifits for many years.

13C: Using Correct Spelling

Directions: Cross out each misspelled word in the following paragraph and write the corrected version above.

Example: History Magazine features ~~allot~~ ***a lot*** of information about interesting events in the ~~passed~~ ***past***.

I thaught I new allot of information about passed events, but every time that I reed *History Magazine*, I learn how much I really don't no. A recent issue contained articles on historical people and events ranging from Buffalo Bill and Annie Oakley to Charles Dickens, the Jesuits, the history of banilla, and the decade of the 1470s. I was especially intrested in the artical on Buffalo Bill, who always featured real Indians, cowboys and vaqueros, calvarymen and buffaloe soldiers in his Wild West shows, as well as expert shots like Annie Oakley. It's hard to beleive how well she could shoot, considering the fairely primitive technology of the late 1800s and early 1900s. Buffalo Bill, who's actual name was William Frederick Cody, complemented her by giving her the nickname "Little Sure Shot." Once, while the show was touring in Europe, Annie Oakley shot the tip off of a cigarret held by Kaiser Wilhelm II. Biger than a circus and with more than a hundred hourses, more than six acres were needed for all of the demonstrations and exhibitions that where included in the show. Beside battles, rideing demonstrations, amazing stunts, and shooting exibitions, there was an Indian village and a cowboy camp, and food was avalable for sale from "Buffalo Bill's Caterer." Somtimes just reading about an exiting time can make me feel like I was really their.

14A: Using Commas in a Series

Directions: Add commas where they are needed in several series in the paragraph below. Other commas are already provided.

Example: Yahoo Webcrawler Dogpile and Google are examples of the many different search engines available on the Internet.

Corrected: *Yahoo, Webcrawler, Dogpile, and Google are examples of the many different search engines available on the Internet.*

There is such a large quantity of information available on the Internet these days that it is becoming very difficult to find the exact information we need. People looking for information about a baseball team's schedule may have to wade through vast amounts of local news financial disclosures or player statistics before they hit on the team's home page, and when I recently looked up podiatry osteopathy dentistry and chiropractic, I was overwhelmed with information that I didn't need. Fortunately, there are some strategies that can help searchers find what they are looking for. These include using advanced search features multi-engine searches or plain English searches. Advanced features permit a searcher to specify exact phrases that must be included, as well as words or phrases that must not be included, while multi-engine searches like Dogpile Mamma and SavvySearch allow the user to search several sites at the same time. Natural language search engines such as Answers.com allow searchers to type in a question in plain English. Using one of these strategies the next time you are searching for information on the Internet may help you find the information you want.

14B: Using Commas with Conjunctions and Nonrestrictive Elements

Directions: Add commas where they are needed with conjunctions and nonrestrictive elements in the paragraph below.

Example: Science fiction includes a wide variety of stories but most people have read only one or two styles of science fiction.

Corrected: *Science fiction includes a wide variety of stories, but most people have read only one or two styles of science fiction.*

      Science fiction books and movies have become very popular in recent years. Most science fiction falls into four categories—hard science fiction, science fantasy (also known as sword and sorcery), speculative fiction, and genre science fiction. While hard science fiction features such possible technological advancements as interstellar travel or death rays speculative fiction focuses more on the nature of possible future societies. Although story lines in science fantasy are often modeled after romantic stories of knights in shining armor some science fantasy can be quite original. Genre science fiction which includes the popular *Star Trek* stories takes place in pre-defined but somewhat flexible settings and involves familiar characters and locations such as Captain Kirk and the Starship *Enterprise*. One recent style of science fiction cyberpunk combines elements from several of these categories to portray the interaction of the human mind with computers and these stories often include a streetwise hero or heroes.

14C: Using Commas Correctly

Directions: Add commas where they are needed in the paragraph below.

Example: More than forty years after his death Dr. Martin Luther King Jr. is still honored and remembered.

Corrected: *More than forty years after his death, Dr. Martin Luther King, Jr., is still honored and remembered.*

Beginning on January 20 1986 the third Monday in January has been designated as a national holiday to honor Dr. Martin Luther King Jr. whose leadership and vision have inspired generations of Americans. King was born in Atlanta Georgia in 1929 and he began studying at Morehouse College in Atlanta when he was only fifteen. After he graduated from Morehouse he became a prominent figure in the civil rights movement advocating nonviolent forms of protest against segregation. As pastor of a Baptist church in Montgomery Alabama King was instrumental in organizing the black community to boycott Montgomery's bus system which was racially segregated. Following the 13-month boycott laws were eventually passed to make segregation unlawful in transportation education and public facilities. King is well-known for his "I have a dream" speech which he delivered in 1963 during a peaceful demonstration and march in Washington D. C. Awarded the Nobel Peace Prize in 1964 King was the youngest person ever to receive this honor. When he was only thirty-nine years old King was assassinated by a sniper in Memphis where he had gone to support striking city workers.

14D: Using Commas Correctly

Directions: Add commas where they are needed in the paragraph below.

Example: Sports fans keep track of statistics injuries and personal lives of their favorite players.

Corrected: *Sports fans keep track of statistics, injuries, and personal lives of their favorite players.*

Baseball football soccer rugby and other team sports have thousands of dedicated fans. Many spend hundreds or even thousands of dollars each year to pay for season tickets and travel to away games as well as to purchase shirts jackets caps and other items featuring the team logo or honoring outstanding players. Even if their team does not perform well most people stay loyal to the team throughout the season. Identification with your team becomes very important so you put a lot of energy into cheering them on to victory. If others think your team is unworthy then you may feel unworthy yourself but when your team is winning you feel as if you are also a winner. Although competition between opposing teams is usually sportsmanlike extreme fans have been known to call each other names get into fights and actually injure each other. However this type of behavior is not common. For most people choosing a team and remaining loyal to it is a healthy positive experience. They bond with other fans enjoy watching games together and experience the thrill of winning.

15A: Using Quotation Marks

Directions: Add quotation marks where they are needed in the paragraph below.

Example: Bob Dylan's Blowin' In the Wind is still one of my favorite songs.

Corrected: *Bob Dylan's "Blowin' In the Wind" is still one of my favorite songs.*

How long have you been a student at this college? I asked the person sitting next to me on the first day of a music appreciation class. Two years, he replied, and then asked me if I had heard anything about the class. Yes, and I'm a little nervous, I answered him. I've heard that we study everything from classical music like Bach's Christmas Oratorio and Mozart's Eine Kleine Nachtmusik to gospel, rhythm and blues, plus modern types of rock music like rap, techno, and punk. Yes, he responded, and we'll spend a lot of time listening to music in class. That will be great, I continued, but I'm afraid I'll never to able to identify all those different kinds of music and different composers to pass the tests. I don't know my Bach from my Beethoven. No problem, my classmate insisted, you can check out all the tapes or CDs from the library and listen to them over and over until you've got it. That's a relief, and thanks for the encouragement, I whispered to him as music started to play and the instructor approached the podium, waved her arms in the air enthusiastically, and shouted, Good morning, music lovers!

15B: Using Apostrophes

Directions: Add apostrophes where they are needed in the paragraph below.

Example: Tom and Kathleens bikes both need to be adjusted.

Corrected: *Tom's and Kathleen's bikes both need to be adjusted.*

One of my favorite activities is riding a mountain bike on nearby paths and trails. My bike works well even though its a few years old. My bike isnt as fancy as my friends bike, but it gets the job done. My friend Louis Carrillos bike has more features, like front suspension and V-brakes, but my bikes frame is stronger and it has decent components too. Both bikes tires are designed for off-road riding, and we carry patch kits to repair any flats we get. Both are mens bikes, with high top bars on the frames. Of course, womens mountain bikes are available too, and mountain biking is becoming more and more popular as a womens sport. A bikes seat design should be different for a woman because a womans bone structure and weight distribution are different than a mans. My favorite place to ride is in the Laguna Mountains, although I dont have as much time to ride as I did when I was younger. If you decide to take up riding, make sure that your bike is a good fit for you, and that the handlebars arent too high or too low for comfort. Also, be sure to wear a helmet and gloves to protect yourself in a crash; one day youll be thankful you have them.

15C: Using Apostrophes and Capitalization

Directions: Add apostrophes where they are needed in the paragraph below, and correct any mistakes in capitalization.

Example: just a few miles East of town is the citys newest and most impressive shopping center.

Corrected: ***Just*** *a few miles* ***east*** *of town is the* ***city's*** *newest and most impressive shopping center.*

laguna ranch town center isn't like any of the other nearby shopping malls. according to its developers, its a "lifestyle center" rather than just a shopping center. each store and restaurant features its own unique design. the center doesnt have any identical buildings or "cloned" storefronts. to create the feel of small town shopping, the main streets have parking spaces right in front of the stores. one thing youll love about shopping there is that its often possible to park right in front of your favorite store, such as macys, chicos, sharper image, ann taylor, or anthropologie. if youre an early shopper and arrive before 10:00 a.m., youll have your choice of convenient parking places. would you like to walk your jack russell terrier or your bullmastiff before or after shopping? thats easy. theres a dog park at the West end of the Center where dogs can stroll or run with their owners, followed by a drink from one of the doggy water dishes near the entrances of the stores. Add colorful flowers, park benches along the streets, two outdoor fireplaces with chairs where shoppers can relax, and now the scenes complete.

15D: Using Semicolons and Colons

Directions: Add semicolons and colons where they are needed in the paragraph below. Do not add any other types of punctuation.

Example: Princess Matoaka was the daughter of Chief Powhatan she is more commonly known by her nickname, Pocahontas.

Correct: *Princess Matoaka was the daughter of Chief Powhatan; she is more commonly known by her nickname, Pocahontas.*

There are many stories and legends but few historical records about Pocahontas and Captain John Smith. Some claim they were lovers others say they were close platonic friends. Pocahontas helped Smith and other settlers of the Jamestown colony on a number of different occasions she saved Smith from being executed by Chief Powhatan, she risked her life to warn the colonists of an ambush, and she brought venison and other supplies to the colonists after a fire had nearly burned them out. Without Pocahontas, the colony in Jamestown, Virginia, might not have survived the history of British colonization in America might have been very different. After Smith returned to England, a wealthy planter named John Rolfe fell in love with Pocahontas. The two of them were married and had a son Smith, however, never married. When Pocahontas and John Smith finally saw each other again in England, their meeting was stormy. She was angry about several things his long absence from Jamestown, his failure to send word to her, and his betrayal of her people.